How Do You Like Your Eggs?
Crack Into Your Personality, Yolk and All
Copyright © 2025 by Dr. Constance Santego

Published by Maximillian Enterprises
Interior Design & Layout by Constance Santego

Soft Cover ISBN: 978-1-990062-83-4
eBook ISBN: 978-1-990062-84-1

Published, printed, and bound in the United States of America

No eggs were harmed in the making of this book
(except the scrambled ones). ◯

HOW DO YOU LIKE YOUR EGGS?

Crack Into Your Personality, Yolk and All
By Dr. Constance Santego

Dedication

*For all the eggs in the carton—
the scrambled, the sunny, the deviled,
and the golden.*

Because the world needs every flavor of you.

How Do You Like Your Eggs?

Every morning, millions of people answer the same question without even thinking: *How do you like your eggs?*

Sunny side up? Scrambled? Poached? Hard-boiled? Each choice feels small, yet it says something about you. Eggs, after all, are more than breakfast. They're symbols of beginnings, creativity, and possibility—tiny packages of potential, wrapped in a shell.

This book is a playful journey into personality, cracked open one egg at a time. You'll discover which egg best matches your vibe, what that says about your strengths and quirks, and even which other "eggs" you pair well with.

So grab a fork (or a spoon), turn the page, and get ready to find out: *Which egg are you?*

◯ Raw Egg Personality

You're bold, daring, and unfiltered—just like a raw egg straight from the shell. You're not afraid to take risks or show up as your most authentic self. Some people might find you intense or unconventional, but those who appreciate your raw energy know you bring freshness and truth wherever you go.

Strengths:

- Courageous and adventurous
- Authentic and honest
- Brings fresh energy to any space

Quirks:

- Can feel "too much" for some people
- Sometimes reckless with risks
- Vulnerable when not handled with care

✓ Best Served With: A shot of espresso (bold meets bold)
✓ Carton Buddy: Sunny Side Up (helps soften your edges)
✓ Watch Out For: Fabergé Egg (they think you're "too messy")

Your Motto:

"No shell, no filter, just me."

○ Hard-Boiled Egg Personality

Solid. Reliable. Unshakable. Just like a hard-boiled egg, you're practical and straightforward, with no frills or fuss. People can count on you—you show up, get the job done, and keep things steady when life gets messy. You might not always reveal your softer side right away, but it's there, waiting for those who take the time to know you.

Strengths:

- Loyal and dependable
- Calm under pressure
- Great at keeping life simple and steady

Quirks:

- Can come off a little "closed off"
- Prefers routine over change
- Sometimes forgets to let your softer side show

✓ Best Served With: A sprinkle of salt and pepper — classic, no frills.
✓ Carton Buddy: Soft-Boiled Egg (balances out your tough shell with tenderness).
✓ Watch Out For: Sunny Side Up (your realism clashes with their relentless optimism).

◯ Soft-Boiled Egg Personality

Gentle, comforting, and just a little fragile—you're the soft-boiled egg. You carry a tender heart and a nurturing nature, offering warmth and care to those you love. People find comfort in your presence, though sometimes they don't realize how much you need protection, too.

Strengths:

- Compassionate and nurturing
- Brings comfort and emotional warmth
- Sensitive to the needs of others

Quirks:

- Can be easily hurt or overwhelmed
- Sometimes struggles with boundaries
- May rely on others for reassurance

- ✓ Best Served With: Toast soldiers — gentle support to dip into.
- ✓ Carton Buddy: Hard-Boiled Egg (protective shell meets tender heart).
- ✓ Watch Out For: Deviled Egg (their teasing may bruise your soft center).

⬭ Scotch Egg Personality

Protective, bold, and hearty—you're the Scotch egg. With a tough outer layer and a strong presence, you guard what matters most and aren't afraid to take up space. Inside, though, lies a steady, dependable core that people can always trust. You thrive in challenges and bring strength and reassurance to those around you.

Strengths:

- Protective and loyal
- Bold, confident, and courageous
- Provides comfort and strength in tough times

Quirks:

- Can be a little intimidating at first
- Sometimes hides vulnerability behind a strong exterior
- May resist showing your softer side

- ✓ Best Served With: A pint of beer — hearty, bold, and unapologetic.
- ✓ Carton Buddy: Soft-Boiled Egg (adores your protective shell and feels safe with you).
- ✓ Watch Out For: Over-Easy Egg (your intensity may smother their chill vibe).

Wrapped in Ham and Bread Crumbs

⬭ Deviled Egg Personality

Playful, witty, and always ready to spice things up—you're the life of the party. Like a platter of deviled eggs at a gathering, people can't resist you. You add flavor to every situation and have a mischievous streak that keeps others guessing.

Strengths:

- Quick-witted and entertaining
- Charms people with ease
- Brings fun to any event

Quirks:

- Can be a little too cheeky at times
- Doesn't always take things seriously
- Tends to stir the pot just for excitement

✓ Best Served With: Paprika on top and a crowd to entertain.
✓ Carton Buddy: Scrambled Egg (together, you're chaos and comedy gold).
✓ Watch Out For: Poached Egg (they'll get stressed by your mischief).

◯ Pickled Egg Personality

Quirky, tangy, and full of zest—you're the pickled egg. You stand out in the crowd with your sharp wit and unique style. Some people might raise an eyebrow at first, but once they get to know you, they realize you bring excitement, flavor, and a refreshing twist to life.

Strengths:

- Bold and memorable
- Brings energy and spark to any situation
- Willing to take risks and be different

Quirks:

- Can be a little too intense for some
- Not always everyone's "taste"
- May struggle with being misunderstood

- ✓ Best Served With: A pint of ale — tangy, quirky, and unforgettable.
- ✓ Carton Buddy: Deviled Egg (partners in playful mischief and spice).
- ✓ Watch Out For: Meringue (your sharp tang may overwhelm their delicate sweetness).

Your Motto:
"Why blend in when you can stand out?"

◯ Sunny Side Up Personality

Bright, warm, and always looking on the bright side—you're the morning sun on a plate. People are naturally drawn to your optimism and open-hearted nature. You see possibilities where others see problems, and you believe a smile can fix almost anything.

Strengths:

- Radiates positivity and encouragement
- Makes people feel comfortable and valued
- Brings light into even the gloomiest moments

Quirks:

- Can be overly trusting
- Sometimes avoids conflict by "staying sunny"
- Tends to wear your heart on your sleeve

- ✓ Best Served With: Fresh orange juice — bright, cheerful, and full of zest.
- ✓ Carton Buddy: Omelette (they love your optimism, and you adore their variety).
- ✓ Watch Out For: Hard-Boiled Egg (your sunshine feels wasted on their unyielding shell).

◯ Over-Easy Egg Personality

Gentle, balanced, and a little bit of both—you're the over-easy egg. You know how to go with the flow, and you don't get ruffled easily. People appreciate your calm presence and your ability to see both sides of a situation. You're smooth, approachable, and quietly dependable, with just the right amount of softness inside.

Strengths:

- Adaptable and easygoing
- Mediator who brings balance to groups
- Approachable and comforting

Quirks:

- Sometimes avoids making firm decisions
- Can downplay your own needs for others' comfort
- May hold back your deeper feelings

✓ Best Served With: A side of crispy bacon — easygoing, classic, and always welcome.
✓ Carton Buddy: Cloud Egg (your calm keeps their dreaminess grounded).
✓ Watch Out For: Scotch Egg (their intensity can smother your chill vibe).

Your Motto:
"Take it easy—it'll all work out."

◯ Over-Hard Egg Personality

Practical, steady, and no-nonsense—you're the over-hard egg. You like things clear, consistent, and well done. People know they can count on you to be thorough and dependable, even if you don't always show your softer side. You bring order where there's chaos and make sure nothing is left half-finished.

Strengths:

- Reliable and hardworking
- Straightforward and dependable
- Values structure and clarity

Quirks:

- Can come across as rigid or overly serious
- Struggles with spontaneity
- May hide emotions beneath a tough surface

✓ Best Served With: Black coffee — straightforward, no nonsense.
✓ Carton Buddy: Hard-Boiled Egg (you respect each other's structure and consistency).
✓ Watch Out For: Cloud Egg (their whimsy makes you roll your eyes).

◯ Poached Egg Personality

Graceful, delicate, and refined—you're the elegant one of the bunch. Like a poached egg, you have a soft center and a gentle way of moving through the world. People admire your calm presence and sense of balance. You notice beauty in small things and often create harmony wherever you go.

Strengths:

- Thoughtful and sensitive to others' needs
- Brings peace and calm to stressful situations
- Appreciates subtlety and depth

Quirks:

- Can be overly cautious or hesitant
- Sometimes hard for others to "get to know" you fully
- May avoid the messiness of conflict

- ✓ Best Served With: A slice of sourdough — refined and understated.
- ✓ Carton Buddy: Quiche (you both value comfort and subtle elegance).
- ✓ Watch Out For: Deviled Egg (their wild spice unsettles your calm refinement).

Your Motto:
"Stay soft, even in a hard world."

◯ Eggs Benedict Personality

Sophisticated, stylish, and a little indulgent—you're the Eggs Benedict of the carton. You enjoy the finer things in life and aren't afraid to treat yourself. People see you as polished and composed, but those close to you know you also have a warm, comforting side. You value quality over quantity and bring a sense of elegance to any occasion.

Strengths:

- Refined taste and thoughtful presence
- Balances comfort with class
- Inspires others to elevate their own standards

Quirks:

- Can come across as a bit high-maintenance
- Prefers structure and order over spontaneity
- Sometimes forgets to relax and be "messy"

✓ Best Served With: Champagne — elegant, indulgent, and a little extra.
✓ Carton Buddy: Fabergé Egg (together, you're the luxe power pair).
✓ Watch Out For: Raw Egg (their messy boldness ruins your polished vibe).

◯ Scrambled Egg Personality

You're lively, spontaneous, and a little unpredictable—just like scrambled eggs sizzling in the pan. People love your playful energy and your ability to make any moment fun. You're quick to adapt, whether life hands you salt, pepper, or a dash of hot sauce.

Strengths:

- Creative and open-minded
- Can adapt quickly to change
- Brings joy and laughter wherever you go

Quirks:

- Sometimes, scatter your energy in too many directions
- Can be impulsive, leaping before you look
- Not always great at sticking with one thing

- ✓ Best Served With: Bottomless mimosas — chaotic, bubbly, and fun.
- ✓ Carton Buddy: Deviled Egg (together, you're the life of the party).
- ✓ Watch Out For: Egg White Omelette (they think you're way too messy).

Your Motto:
"Why be neat when you can be fun?"

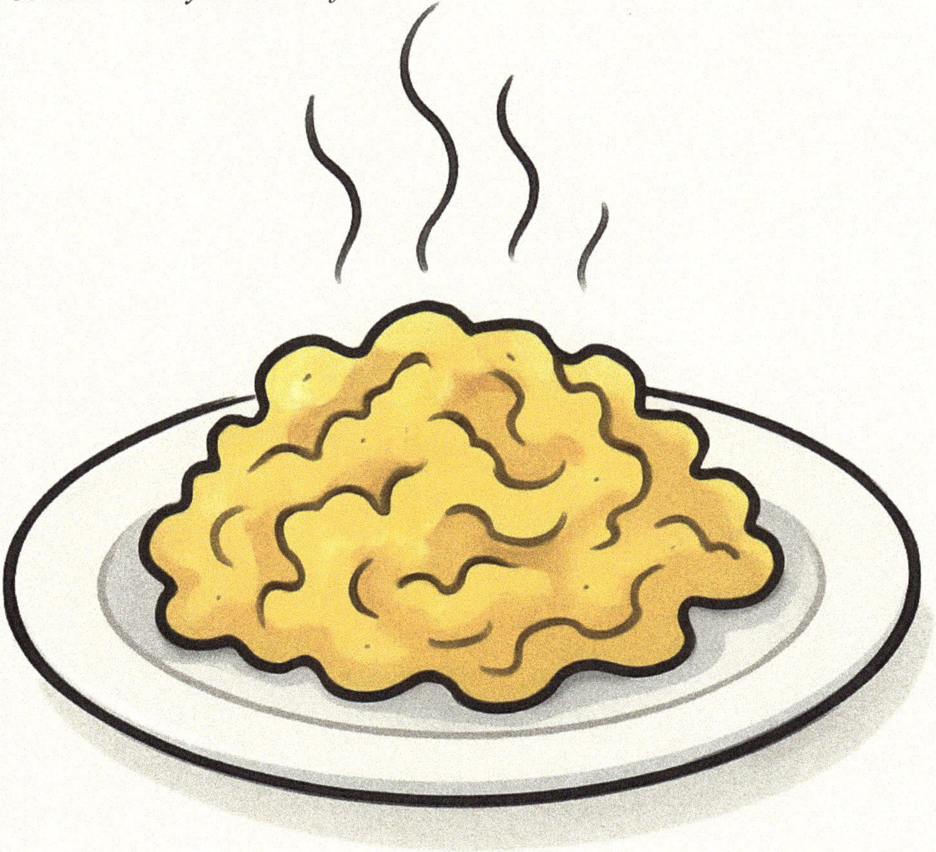

⬯ Egg White Omelette Personality

Disciplined, focused, and health-conscious—you're the egg white omelette of the carton. You set goals and stick to them, often inspiring others with your commitment to wellness and self-improvement. You're clear about your priorities and know how to cut out the "extras" that don't serve your bigger vision.

Strengths:

- Dedicated and hardworking
- Health-minded and goal-oriented
- Inspires others through example

Quirks:

- Can be a little too strict or rigid at times
- Sometimes forgets to indulge or have fun
- May judge yourself (and others) too harshly

- ✓ Best Served With: A green smoothie — lean, clean, and disciplined.
- ✓ Carton Buddy: Over-Hard Egg (you both love structure and consistency).
- ✓ Watch Out For: Scrambled Egg (their chaos throws off your routine).

◯ Omelette Personality

Layered, versatile, and full of surprises—you're the omelette of the bunch. Just as an omelette can hold endless fillings, you carry many passions, talents, and ideas within you. You thrive when juggling different projects and love adding variety to your life.

Strengths:

- Multifaceted and resourceful
- Can adapt to many roles and environments
- Brings together different people and ideas with ease

Quirks:

- Sometimes you spread yourself too thin
- Can struggle to focus on just one path
- Prone to overstuffing your schedule (like an overloaded omelette!)

- ✓ Best Served With: A side of hash browns — versatile, hearty, and satisfying.
- ✓ Carton Buddy: Sunny Side Up (their optimism fuels your variety).
- ✓ Watch Out For: Century Egg (your restless energy may not sync with their slow depth).

◯ Frittata Personality

Hearty, dependable, and always ready to share—you're the frittata of the carton. You thrive in groups and love bringing people together. Like a baked omelette packed with layers of flavor, you're full of substance, warmth, and reliability. People know they can count on you to provide comfort and support when it's needed most.

Strengths:

- Loyal and dependable friend
- Nurturing and generous with time and energy
- Brings people together with ease

Quirks:

- Can sometimes put others' needs before your own
- May be seen as predictable or too steady
- Struggles to step out of your comfort zone

- ✓ Best Served With: A fresh garden salad — wholesome, hearty, and nourishing.
- ✓ Carton Buddy: Quiche (you're both comfort-focused and community-minded).
- ✓ Watch Out For: Raw Egg (their recklessness disrupts your dependable vibe).

◯ Quiche Personality

Warm, comforting, and indulgent—you're the quiche of the carton. You bring people together with a sense of care and nourishment, offering comfort when it's needed most. Like a rich and savory quiche filled with layers of goodness, you have depth, heart, and a way of making people feel at home.

Strengths:

- Nurturing and family-oriented
- Creates a sense of comfort and belonging
- Reliable, with a generous spirit

Quirks:

- Can sometimes give too much of yourself
- May struggle to put your own needs first
- Occasionally resists change to protect tradition

✓ Best Served With: A cozy cup of tea — warm, comforting, and nurturing.
✓ Carton Buddy: Frittata (together, you're the comfort couple of the carton).
✓ Watch Out For: Pickled Egg (their sharp tang can unsettle your gentle nature).

◯ Cloud Egg Personality

Dreamy, whimsical, and full of wonder—you're the cloud egg. Your head may be in the clouds, but your heart is always in the right place. You see beauty in everything and inspire others to look beyond the ordinary. Like whipped whites with a golden yolk nestled in the center, you bring both softness and light wherever you go.

Strengths:

- Imaginative and visionary
- Brings inspiration and hope to others
- Gentle and uplifting presence

Quirks:

- Can be a little too idealistic at times
- Struggles with staying grounded
- May drift away from practical details

- ✓ Best Served With: A vanilla latte — light, dreamy, and comforting.
- ✓ Carton Buddy: Over-Easy Egg (their calm steadiness keeps you grounded).
- ✓ Watch Out For: Over-Hard Egg (they'll dismiss your whimsy as unrealistic).

◯ Meringue Egg Personality

Light, airy, and delightfully sweet—you're the meringue of the carton. You have a way of lifting people's spirits and making life feel softer, brighter, and more fun. People love your charm and your ability to turn even the simplest moment into something special.

Strengths:

- Uplifting and joyful
- Creative with a flair for beauty
- Brings lightness to heavy situations

Quirks:

- Can be a bit too delicate under pressure
- Sometimes, prioritize appearance over substance
- May avoid conflict to keep things "sweet"

✓ Best Served With: Fresh berries — light, sweet, and full of charm.
✓ Carton Buddy: Cloud Egg (together, you float through life in whimsy and wonder).
✓ Watch Out For: Pickled Egg (their tang may overwhelm your delicate sweetness).

⬯ Easter Egg Personality

Colorful, playful, and full of surprises—you're the Easter Egg of the bunch. You delight in bringing joy to others, whether through creativity, humor, or unexpected little gifts of kindness. Beneath your bright exterior lies depth, and people love discovering the layers of who you are.

Strengths:

- Playful and imaginative
- Brings delight and wonder to those around you
- Surprising depth beyond your cheerful exterior

Quirks:

- Sometimes hard for others to "see the real you"
- Can feel scattered when chasing too many fun ideas
- May hide your deeper feelings behind a cheerful mask

- ✓ Best Served With: A basket of surprises — playful, colorful, and full of fun.
- ✓ Carton Buddy: Sunny Side Up (your joy multiplies when paired together).
- ✓ Watch Out For: Hard-Boiled Egg (they may find your playfulness a little childish).

◯ Century Egg Personality

Mysterious, profound, and unlike anyone else—you're the century egg. At first, people may not understand you, but those who take the time to appreciate your depth find you unforgettable. You carry wisdom beyond your years, with a perspective that stretches far beyond the surface.

Strengths:

- Deep thinker with old-soul energy
- Offers unique insights that others overlook
- Patient and steady, not swayed by trends

Quirks:

- Can be misunderstood or judged too quickly
- Sometimes, keep your true self hidden
- May feel "out of step" with the modern pace of life

- ✓ Best Served With: A pot of jasmine tea — patient, refined, and timeless.
- ✓ Carton Buddy: Golden Egg (your wisdom complements their ambitious vision).
- ✓ Watch Out For: Omelette (their restless energy may clash with your slow depth).

Your Motto:

"Time reveals true flavor."

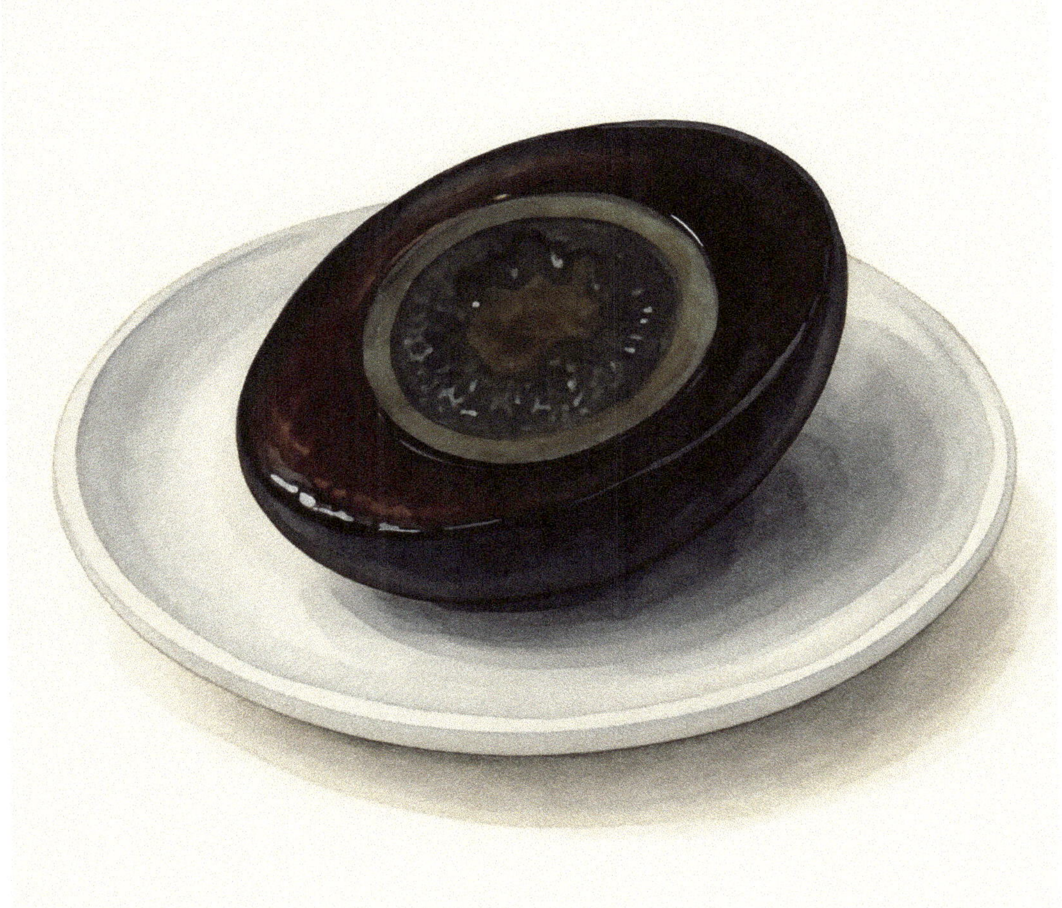

○ Fabergé Egg Personality

Glamorous, rare, and unforgettable—you're the Fabergé egg. You're not about what's on the plate, but about the story, the artistry, and the wow factor. People admire your elegance and the way you shine in a crowd. You remind others that life isn't just about survival—it's about beauty, meaning, and treasures worth keeping.

Strengths:

- Radiates elegance and charm
- Inspires awe and admiration
- Symbol of creativity, uniqueness, and legacy

Quirks:

- Can seem untouchable or intimidating
- Sometimes mistaken for being "all show"
- May struggle to relax or let down your guard

- ✓ Best Served With: A glass of champagne — sparkling, elegant, and rare.
- ✓ Carton Buddy: Eggs Benedict (your luxe tastes make you the power pair).
- ✓ Watch Out For: Raw Egg (their messy boldness disrupts your polished shine).

◯ Golden Egg Personality

Ambitious, visionary, and radiant—you're the golden egg. You dream big and see possibilities where others see limits. People admire your confidence and your ability to inspire others to reach higher. You're rare, valuable, and you shine brightest when you're chasing your purpose.

Strengths:

- Big-picture thinker and innovator
- Inspires others with bold ideas
- Charismatic and naturally motivating

Quirks:

- Can feel pressure to "always succeed"
- Sometimes overlooks small details in pursuit of big goals
- May struggle with perfectionism or fear of losing your shine

✓ Best Served With: Truffle toast — ambitious, rare, and indulgent.
✓ Carton Buddy: Century Egg (your vision shines brighter with their wisdom).
✓ Watch Out For: Scrambled Egg (their scattered chaos distracts your focus).

Your Motto:
"Greatness begins within."

EGG WELLNESS GUIDE

HEALTH

⬭ Egg Wellness Guide: How Each Egg Stays Healthy

The Strong Shells (Grounded & Practical Health)

- **Hard-Boiled Egg** → *Steady & strong.* Thrives on routine, balanced meals, and early bedtimes. Needs to remember to show emotions, not just hold them in.
- **Over-Hard Egg** → *Tough exterior.* Loves structure (gym schedules, vitamins on time). Risks of burnout if they never relax.
- **Frittata** → *Hearty health.* Well-fed by community and routine. Needs to watch over-committing and neglecting self-care.

The Light & Energetic Eggs (Optimistic Health)

- **Sunny Side Up** → *Powered by positivity.* Mental health thrives on laughter and sunshine. Needs to protect energy from toxic people.
- **Over-Easy Egg** → *Balanced wellness.* Rarely too stressed, but may overlook their own health to keep the peace.
- **Scrambled Egg** → *Chaotic vitality.* Bursts of energy, but needs grounding (hydration, rest) to avoid burnout.

The Gentle & Sensitive Shells (Emotional Health)

- **Soft-Boiled Egg** → *Tender care.* Health is tied to emotions; stress shows quickly. Benefits from safe spaces and gentle routines.
- **Poached Egg** → *Refined health.* Needs calm environments, clean food, and mindfulness. Can be sensitive to overstimulation.
- **Quiche** → *Comfort health.* Nurtures others, but must remember to nurture self. Health improves with cozy rituals and good food.

The Bold & Spicy Eggs (Fiery Health)

- **Deviled Egg** → *Party wellness.* Loves indulgence and late nights. Needs balance to avoid overdoing it. Best when active and laughing.
- **Raw Egg** → *Risky vitality.* Bold in health choices (might try extreme diets or sports). Needs to avoid recklessness.
- **Scotch Egg** → *Protects health.* Strong and sturdy, but must release tension from carrying others' burdens.

The Dreamers & Quirky Shells (Whimsical Health)

- **Cloud Egg** → *Dream body.* Stays healthy through creativity, dance, and lightness. Needs grounding practices (walking, deep breathing).
- **Meringue** → *Sweet wellness.* Health is tied to joy and aesthetics. Can be fragile under pressure, so thrives on gentle self-love.
- **Easter Egg** → *Surprise wellness.* Pops of energy, but easily distracted. Needs consistency in routine.
- **Pickled Egg** → *Zesty body.* Strong in unique ways. Might try quirky remedies; health improves when embracing individuality.

The Rare & Symbolic Shells (Soulful Health)

- **Century Egg** → *Deep-rooted health.* Strong but unusual rhythms. Thrives on patience, slow living, and ancient wisdom.
- **Golden Egg** → *Vital abundance.* Radiates energy when aligned with purpose. Stress comes from perfectionism; needs balance.
- **Fabergé Egg** → *Elegant wellness.* Prioritizes appearance, but true health comes when they care for the inside too.

THE EGGCONOMY

WEALTH BY  PREDICTIONS EGG TYPE

Comfortable, enjoys simple pleasures

Will leave a lasting legacy

Walking on financial eggshells

Expenses are extravagant

◯ The Eggconomy: Wealth Predictions by Egg Type

The Golden Carton (Natural Abundance)

- **Golden Egg** → *Destined for prosperity.* Sees opportunities everywhere and attracts success with big ideas. Likely to build empires or at least own fancy spoons.
- **Fabergé Egg** → *Old money vibes.* Wealth comes through beauty, art, or luxury—an extravagant spender, but also an investment in memories and glamour.
- **Eggs Benedict** → *Comfortable wealth.* Likes refinement, fine dining, and steady streams of income. Attracts abundance by networking and presentation.

The Steady Earners (Practical & Secure)

- **Hard-Boiled Egg** → *Slow and steady.* Builds savings, loves security, and values a retirement plan. May not be flashy, but never cracks under pressure.
- **Over-Hard Egg** → *Works hard, saves harder.* Disciplined with money, prefers stability over risk.
- **Frittata** → *Community builder.* Attracts wealth through teamwork, teaching, or service.

The Risk-Takers (Boom or Bust)

- **Raw Egg** → *The entrepreneur.* Wealth through daring ventures. High risk, high reward. Sometimes wins big, sometimes just… a mess on the floor.
- **Scrambled Egg** → *The hustler.* Juggles multiple streams of income, never boring. May struggle with consistency, but luck often lands them on their feet.
- **Deviled Egg** → *The wildcard.* Attracts money through charm, humor, or entertainment. Wealth flows in when they play to their magnetic energy.

The Comfort Wealth (Modest & Nourishing)

- **Soft-Boiled Egg** → *Nurturer's wealth.* Gains through supportive roles, caregiving, or family. May not chase riches, but finds abundance in emotional security.
- **Quiche** → *Home & hearth prosperity.* Wealth through tradition, family, or food. Always makes sure everyone is fed—literally and financially.
- **Pickled Egg** → *Odd but valuable.* Attracts money in quirky or unexpected ways—side hustles, inventions, or niches others overlook.

The Dreamers & Mystics (Unusual Fortunes)

- **Cloud Egg** → *Dream chaser.* Wealth shows up through creativity, imagination, or spiritual pursuits. Floats into abundance when aligned with vision.
- **Meringue** → *Sweet fortune.* Prosperity is tied to charm, beauty, or artistry. Tends to attract opportunities with lightness and joy.
- **Century Egg** → *Ancient fortune.* Gains wealth over time through patience, wisdom, or unconventional paths. Rarely fast, but deeply rooted.
- **Easter Egg** → *Hidden treasures.* Wealth through surprises, chance opportunities, or luck. Life is full of colorful windfalls.

Compatibility with Wealth

- *Sunny Side Up*: Attracts wealth through optimism and collaboration—good vibes = good fortune.
- *Poached Egg*: Draws abundance in refined, quiet ways. More likely to create wealth through subtle, precise moves.
- *Over-Easy Egg*: Stays balanced with money—rarely rich, rarely broke. Comfortable and content.
- *Scotch Egg*: Gains wealth by protecting others or through bold ventures (law enforcement, defense, leadership).

Egg Dating Guide
Love in the Carton

◯ **Egg Dating Guide:**
Love in the Carton

Welcome to **Dear Carton Counselor**, where your favorite egg personalities write in with their love dilemmas. Let's crack into this week's letters…

Best Matches (Soulmates in the Carton)

Dear Carton Counselor,
I'm a *Sunny Side Up*, always cheerful, always smiling. My new crush is an *Omelette* — they've got a million hobbies and can't sit still! Is this going to work?
— Hopeful in the Frying Pan

> **Dear Hopeful,**
> This is a brunch-made-in-heaven. Your optimism keeps Omelette grounded, while their variety keeps you from getting bored. Expect laughter, shared adventures, and way too many hobbies. Go ahead — host that brunch together.

Dear Carton Counselor,

I'm a *Scrambled*, and my partner is *Deviled*. Together, we're loud, messy, and a little spicy. People say it won't last. Are we doomed?

— Chaotic in Love

> **Dear Chaotic,**
>
> You two are pure trouble — in the very best way. The dance floor? Yours. The punch bowl? Definitely spiked. This may not be forever, but oh yolk, is it fun while it lasts.

Dear Carton Counselor,

I'm *Hard-Boiled*, steady and practical, but my heart belongs to a *Soft-Boiled*. They're tender and fragile. Can opposites attract?

— Sturdy Shell

> **Dear Sturdy,**
>
> Absolutely. You bring the shell, they bring the warmth. Together, you're a balanced breakfast: safe, steady, and oh-so comforting.

Dear Carton Counselor,

I'm an *Eggs Benedict,* and I've started seeing a *Fabergé Egg*. We both love the finer things — Paris, wine tastings, the perfect brunch table. But… people keep saying we're "too extra" together. Are we doomed to be fabulous but lonely?
— Hollandaise Heart

>**Dear Hollandaise,**
>
>Darling, if being "too extra" is wrong, why be right? You and Fabergé are the luxe pair — the couple who posts vacation selfies from Paris and argues about wine notes. High-maintenance? Maybe. But you understand each other's standards, and that's all that matters.

Dear Carton Counselor,

I'm a *Frittata*. Dependable, hearty, always there for the family. I've fallen for a *Quiche*, who's just as comforting and warm as I am. But is it too much of the same thing? Will people think we're boring?
— Hearty but Unsure

>**Dear Hearty,**
>
>Boring? Please. You and Quiche are the comfort couple — the ones who make everyone feel welcome. You're cozy Sundays, family dinners, and warm gatherings. Safe? Yes. Predictable? Maybe. But also deeply loved and never lonely.

Dear Carton Counselor,

I'm a *Century Egg*, full of mystery and patience. My heart's been stolen by a *Golden Egg*, who's all about big visions and future dreams. Can an old soul really mesh with such ambition?

— Ancient Yolk

Dear Ancient,

What a pairing! Your depth balances Golden's sparkle. Together, you're wisdom plus vision — the power couple of the carton. You ground their ambition; they brighten your mystery. It's not just a match… it's a legacy.

Tricky Matches (Could Work… With Effort)

- *Raw Egg writes in about dating Sunny Side Up* → "Sometimes it's magic, sometimes a yolky mess."
- *Egg White Omelette complains about Deviled Egg* → "Stop rolling your eyes and sparks might fly."
- *Pickled Egg dates Hard-Boiled* → "Spice meets stoic — depends who bends."
- *Cloud Egg crushes on Scrambled* → "Fun fling, but needs grounding."
- *Over-Easy with Scotch Egg* → "Could be yin and yang… or just yolk and choke."

Eggsplosive Combos (Handle With Care!)

- *Sunny Side Up writes: "Hard-Boiled keeps calling me unrealistic."* → Expect endless debates.
- *Scrambled & Egg White Omelette try to cohabit* → Confetti + spreadsheets = chaos.
- *Raw Egg & Fabergé Egg try a date* → Oil, vinegar, and cracked shells.
- *Deviled & Poached* → One spills, one cries. Constant drama.
- *Pickled & Meringue* → Cute for one date, never for two.

Secret Crushes (Confessions from the Carton)

- Over-Hard → Cloud Egg: "Wishes they could loosen up."
- Soft-Boiled → Scotch Egg: "Loves the protection."
- Pickled → Deviled: "Two troublemakers, one punch bowl."
- Century → Raw: "Admires the unapologetic boldness."
- Golden → Sunny Side Up: "Big dreams need bright optimism."

⬭ The Last Crack

So, how do you like your eggs? By now, you've probably discovered the yolk that matches your soul — or maybe you realized you're a little scrambled one day, poached the next, with a dash of deviled spice sprinkled in for fun.

That's the beauty of eggs — and people. We're not meant to fit into just one carton. Some of us are hard-boiled steady, others are meringue-light, and a few of us are rare golden finds. And yet, side by side, we make the perfect dozen.

Whether you laughed at your quirks, found comfort in your shell, or spotted your secret crush in another egg, remember this: the world needs all kinds of eggs. Together, we create the omelette of life — rich, messy, colorful, and never boring.

So crack on, stay sunny, and when life gets tough, just remember:
You're egg-xactly who you're meant to be. 🐣

○ **About the Author**

Dr. Constance Santego has been called many things in her life — hard-boiled, scrambled, even a little deviled — but never boring. When she's not cracking open new ideas, she's busy whipping up books on wellness, creativity, and the whimsical side of life.

Like a good omelette, she believes people are best when they mix together all their layers — the sunny, the soft, and the spicy. This book is just one more way she invites readers to find themselves in the carton of life.

She lives in beautiful British Columbia, where she continues to serve up fresh ideas, sunny side up.